The Best in Contemporary BEADWORK

Bead International 2002

The Dairy Barn Cultural Arts Center

Bead International is produced by the Dairy Barn
Southeastern Ohio Cultural Arts Center, Inc., with
major support provided by:

Byzantium, Columbus, Ohio

Miyuki Shoji, Japan

Additional support provided by:

Shipwreck Beads, Olympia, Washington

The Best in Contemporary Beadwork
Bead International 2002

Bead International Program Director: Julie Clark
Book Design: Keith Kneisley
Editor: Nancy Basmajian
Cover artist: Jennifer Maestre, *3 to 1 Twist*
Photography: Karen Wegienek
Additional photography: Azadian, Donna H. Chiarelli, Melinda Holden, Jim Holmes, Joe Manfredini, W. Scott Mitchell, Tom Van Eynde, or provided by the artists as noted.

Library of Congress Cataloging-Publication Data
The Best in Contemporary Beadwork: Bead International, 2002
Produced by the Dairy Barn Cultural Arts Center.
cm.
Includes Index
ISBN 0-971758-1-5
Beadwork—Exhibitions. 2. Glass Beads—Exhibitions. I. Dairy Barn Southeastern Ohio Cultural Arts Center.

Produced by:
Dairy Barn Arts Center
8000 Dairy Lane
P.O. Box 747
Athens, OH 45701
USA

Table of Contents

The Best in Contemporary BEADWORK

Bead International 2002

About The Dairy Barn

The Dairy Barn Southeastern Ohio Cultural Arts Center, located in the beautiful Appalachian foothills, features a full, year-round calendar of exhibits, special activities, and arts education classes for children and adults. The mission of the Dairy Barn is to promote regional, national,

and international arts, crafts, and cultural heritage in Southeastern Ohio, through exhibitions and programs that are unique, educational, family-oriented, and fun. In December 2001, Athens, Ohio—"home of The Dairy Barn Cultural Arts Center"—was named one of the Top Ten Small Arts Towns in the US by *USA Today*.

The history of The Dairy Barn is as colorful as its exhibits. Built in 1914, the structure housed an active dairy herd until the late 1960s. Ten years later, local arts enthusiasts Harriet and Ora Anderson recognized the building's potential as a much needed regional arts center, and they worked tirelessly to rally community support to save the idle, dilapidated structure. With only nine days until the scheduled demolition, the building was saved, and the Dairy Barn Arts Center was born. The building is now on the National Register of Historic Places, and thousands of people visit each year.

Through several renovation projects, the architects have retained the original character of the barn, with the structure evolving from a seasonal, makeshift exhibit space into a first-class, fully accessible arts facility. It includes the 6,500-square-foot Sauber Gallery and the specially equipped Ann Howland Arts Education Center. A $1.5 million renovation and expansion project, completed in 2001, makes the facility a full service arts center, with five new classrooms and a successful Gallery Gift Shop, which showcases the work of regional artists and also artists who exhibit in the Barn's national and international exhibitions.

Two remarkable exhibitions are offered biennially: Quilt National offers the best in contemporary quilts from artists around the world, and Bead International showcases the most innovative artwork in which beads are the primary element. After debuting at The Dairy Barn, these exhibits travel to venues around the country, which broadens the reputation of The Dairy Barn as well as the exhibiting artists. Rounding out the exhibition year are shows that present new artistic expressions and ideas by local and regional artists, as well as youth artists.

One of The Dairy Barn's most successful programs is "Artists in the Schools," in which professional artists are matched with classrooms in schools throughout Athens and surrounding counties to provide arts experiences for youth and new teaching tools for classroom teachers. Thousands of schoolchildren benefit from this program each year.

The Dairy Barn is supported by admissions, memberships, corporate and individual donations, sponsorships, grants, and income from exhibitions. The staff is assisted by a large group of volunteers who annually donate thousands of hours of time and talent.

For a calendar of events and information about other Dairy Barn programs, contact the Dairy Barn Arts Center:
8000 Dairy Lane
P.O. Box 747
Athens, OH 45701

phone 740/592-4981
fax 740/592-5090
email info@dairybarn.org
or visit the web site at http://www.dairybarn.org.

From the Director

Acknowledgments

We wish to thank those who helped make this beautiful exhibition and catalog possible.

First, we must thank the many artists who submitted work, making the job of this year's jury a tough one. The jury consisted of artists Valerie Hector (Chicago) and Mimi Holmes (Minneapolis), and Ruth Summers, Executive Director of the Southern Highland Craft Guild in Asheville, North Carolina. Their expertise brought insights to the process and depth to the exhibition. We thank them for the many hours they devoted to selecting this year's show, and hope they enjoyed the experience as much as we did.

We are deeply appreciative of our exhibition sponsors who have joined us in presenting Bead International: Miyuki Shoji Co., Ltd., of Japan; Byzantium of Columbus, Ohio; Shipwreck Beads of Olympia, Washington; The Ohio Arts Council; and the City of Athens.

We are also appreciative of the support for this, our first self-published catalog, from Beads & Things in Athens, Ohio, The Great Lakes Beadworkers Guild in Royal Oak , Michigan, and the Bead Society of Greater Chicago.

Many thanks to Julie Clark and all of the Dairy Barn staff and volunteers who make this remarkable exhibition possible.

At the conclusion of the exhibition period in Athens, the show is available to travel to venues throughout the country. For more information, call 740 / 594-4981, or e-mail: info@dairybarn.org.

I invite you to visit the Dairy Barn during this and other exhibitions or programs. You won't be disappointed!

Krista Campbell
Executive Director
The Dairy Barn

Jurors' Statements
Bead International 2002

Mimi Holmes

Juror's Statement

After being juried into the past two Bead Internationals, I looked forward to being a juror myself and viewing the array of works. And not being much of a traveler anymore, I was delighted to meet my co-jurors Valerie Hector and Ruth Summers and the capable staff of the venerable Dairy Barn. It is good to wrestle verbally with other jurors on aesthetic issues! Three jurors contribute a wider experience and knowledge base, which in turn yield a wider range of works included in the exhibition. We had no difficulty deciding the Best of Show Award, and Juror's Awards also came quickly.

Homunculus, 19 x 13 in.
Photos: provided by artist

Quality of slides is still an issue. If your slides don't adequately represent your work, the jurors can't imagine what it might really be like. Another concern is that, for whatever reason, most past jurors and other established names in the bead world didn't enter this year.

When jurying bead shows, I am struck by the number of works with a humorous bent. I believe the proportion is much higher in our field. Works ranged from the obvious humor of *"Are You Being Served?,"* *Summer in Fargo, On the Prowl,* and *Female Armor* to the more subtle explorations of *A Present for Hester.*

Great exploration is continuing in the three-dimensional figure (insects, animals, and humans); but I was most impressed with new levels of verisimilitude in the two-dimensional plane. Laura Willits has been in a category of her own for years with her haunting night scenes, and the works of Colleen O'Rourke, Nancy Terry Hooten, and Lisa Lew are achieving great mastery as well as an individualized vision.

Here's to another great Bead International and to all those who continue to work with beads! And count on me to enter my works in the 2004 exhibition!

Mimi Holmes
Artist, writer, and educator

Ruth T. Summers

As jurors for Bead International, we were given one prerequisite for works to be included in the exhibition: "a bead is defined as a pierced object." Artists' interpretations of what constitutes a pierced object were diverse, thus providing a rich variety not only for the jurors but also for viewers of the exhibition.

As an arts administrator, not a working artist, my experience has been honed through years spent curating, jurying, buying, and looking at thousands and thousands of objects each year. When I look at an object, my approach is most likely totally different from that of an artist. Artists tend to be concerned initially with technique. For me, an object must first successfully answer the following questions: Does the piece hold together visually? What is the aesthetic value? Does the overall design work? Is the function appropriate to the piece?

Only then would I consider the technique. To me craftsmanship and mastery of skill is the hallmark of a true artist. Many of the individuals in Bead International have reached a mastery of skill realized by international native cultures that have used beadwork for centuries in ceremonial and decorative objects. Bead International pays homage to this artistry and skill.

In selecting the works included in Bead International, each of us jurors scored entries individually in the early elimination rounds; later we had the opportunity to discuss submissions, and we collectively agreed on the objects for this year's exhibition. This would have been a daunting task for one individual; therefore, the objects included in the exhibition represent a culmination of our combined knowledge.

Works chosen reflect decorative wall pieces, free-standing sculptural works, and items for personal adornment such as clothing and necklaces. Bead artists also have a healthy sense of humor, and many pieces reflect their makers' lively sense of childlike wonder. Of special note in this category is the work of Valorie Harlow, *On the Prowl*, an exceptionally humorous example of a spiffy roadster driven by a very confident dog. Harlow is not only adept at capturing the moment but has created a sculpture entirely covered, down to the wheel spokes, with beads. Harlow is represented with a second piece, *On Dragon's Wings*, a sculpture of a long, fair-haired damsel caught up in a fairy-tale ride on a friendly dragon, small in scale but monumental in mastery of technique.

Ann Citron is represented with two works, *Metatron—Soul on Fire* and *Cat's Cradle*, both multimedia soft sculptures. Citron is able to capture a movement frozen in time and transport the viewer into another realm, a dreamlike dance of half-animal and half-human. The beaded faces are a small part of the overall impact of these pieces.

Nancy Terry Hooten is represented with *I'm All Right,* a complex framed wall piece. Hooten has captured a spring morning; a gentle breeze blows through the lace curtains. The skeleton, sitting on the sofa, was at first off-putting, but the title creates a contradiction. We are left to wonder—are we looking at a self-portrait? Maybe the artist is making a statement referring to her own mortality, not having enough time to bead.

> **"Bead International has more than met its mission of introducing the work of bead artists to a larger audience. ... As for me, I will never look at beads in the same way again."**

Hooten's second piece, *A Present for Hester,* begs more questions: Is this gift of sperm to a friend in need of a donor, or does the box hold something else? Is this another statement about the fragility of the human soul, or has Hester contracted AIDS? The box reveals more than a beaded insignia of the letter A.

Thinking back over the slides and the pieces chosen for this exhibition, I notice that many of the pieces draw not only from nature but hearken back to an earlier era—from the delicate beaded and feather slipper of Susan Etcoff Fraerman and the exquisite blue crocheted ruffle neckpiece by Stephenie Goodwin, to the beaded flora and fauna of Karen Paust, shown in *Tulip Tree & Honey Bee* and *Jack in the Pulpit.* These pieces could be from the Victorian era. Laura Massie Goldberg exemplifies the Victorian ideals of overkill in her peyote-embellished *End Table Base.*

A perfect juxtaposition is the simplified *Little Black Dress* by Nicole Nagel-Gogolak, constructed of black cocktail straws. Ingrid Goldbloom Bloch's *Female Armor* is the ideal garment for long, hot summer evenings—cooled by metal mesh and decorated with nuts, wires, and mesh screen, the ultimate biker bra. Unfortunately "Miss Love" must go barefoot—Ella Johnson-Bentley's *Easy Strider* boot is a miniature.

Bead International has more than met its mission of introducing the work of bead artists to a larger audience. The artists have shared their creativity and innovative techniques; to be recognized as an art form is a challenge. Only time will tell if collectors are willing to support this new art form. As for me, I will never look at beads in the same way again.

Ruth T. Summers
Executive Director
Southern Highland Craft Guild
Asheville, North Carolina

Valerie Hector

True Daring: Reflections on the Contemporary American Beadwork Movement

Barely ten years have passed since *The New Beadwork* (New York: Abrams, 1992) was published. This seminal book staked out a whole new territory in the realm of art history (although some might call it craft history): the contemporary beadwork movement. Most of the pieces featured in this book were made by Americans, working alone in various parts of the country, unaware that they stood at the leading edge of an entirely new movement.

Although plenty of European artists were also exploring the potential of beadwork, they are not so well documented in *The New Beadwork*, for the simple reason that they lived a world away from the authors, Kathlyn Moss and Alice Scherer. Still, the brilliant creations of Viennese artist Jacqueline Lillie did find their way into the book, and we continue to marvel at their astonishing beauty, their radiant mastery of form.

When these *New Beadwork* artists were getting started in the medium, there were far fewer bead stores around, and precious few books devoted wholly to beadwork. Back then, there were only a few teachers offering classes in the medium. Perhaps the most charismatic and influential of them was Joyce Scott of Baltimore.

A decade has gone by, and our movement has begun to mature. Some of the artists featured in *The New Beadwork* have moved on to other pursuits. Others are still going strong. Inspired to some extent by pieces they have seen in *The New Beadwork*, thousands more artists have since joined the medium, and their creative energies continue to propel it forward into uncharted realms. So many new publications are now devoted to beadwork that none of us can keep up. Classes abound, conferences proliferate: a delicious state of affairs!

Already we American beadworkers have had a number of galleries and non-profit organizations both in this country and in other parts of the world featuring our work in individual or group shows. Some of the group shows, such as the Beadz show at the American Craft Museum in 2000, have been impressive and cutting-edge, and designed by sophisticated curators with an international audience in mind.

Yet the Dairy Barn is still the only organization that opens its beautiful exhibition space to us on a regular, biennial basis, and invites well-established jurors to evaluate slide entries for its Bead International shows in a professional environment. But there's more: the Dairy Barn then publishes the work of the selected artists in lavish color books that serve as periodic updates to *The New Beadwork*. While we all like seeing our own pieces in print, we have to recognize that a higher purpose is being served by the Dairy Barn's efforts, which is worth noting here.

Koko Nor Pin, 8 x 3 in.
Photo: provided by artist

The higher purpose is simply this: in a world that still views beadwork past and present with a bit of contempt, the Bead International shows and publications teach us to respect ourselves and our contemporary interpretations of this ancient medium. There is an old adage worth repeating in this context: as we respect ourselves, so others will respect us.

Which brings me to the point of my comments. During the meeting of the jury in the fall of 2001, a worrisome statistic was mentioned. Fewer artists sent applications to The Bead International 2002 than to either of the previous shows. Please don't misunderstand me: there was still an incredible assortment of excellent pieces for us to choose from, and we had to work hard to select the most deserving pieces. We did not always agree—each of us endured some severe disappointment as pieces we admired did not end up in the show. Yes, we certainly had a few heated discussions! But such is the nature of the democratic process.

Yet if this downward trend in applications continues, the Dairy Barn will not be able to go on sponsoring future Bead Internationals. Jurors and Dairy Barn organizers alike noticed a conspicuous absence of applications from more well-established artists—those who have been around for awhile and who have been published more than once in various venues. I cannot exempt myself from their numbers: I confess I have never applied to a Bead International show in the past. Was it fear of rejection? A lack of desire to fill out the forms? Not wanting to spare a piece for a months-long exhibition? Being showed-out? I'm not quite sure.

But I will be applying in the future. And I hope that you will encourage your colleagues, students and friends to apply as well. For there is strength in numbers, and wisdom in small contributions to the well-being of the community. As we know, what goes around, comes around. We can give one another the greatest of gifts: the commitment to excel, and the courage to dare.

Valerie Hector
Artist

The Artwork

Bead International 2002

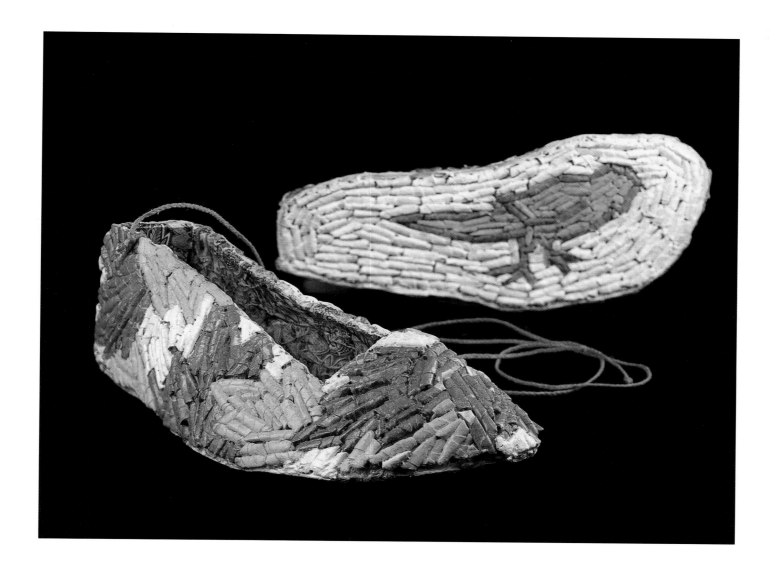

Carolyn Prince Batchelor

Flagstaff, Arizona

Walking in the Garden

9 x 4 x 2 in.
painted and rolled paper, sewn and glued; collage; waxed linen, braided

I wanted to make shoes for an imaginary wearer. The shoes are a commemorative gift for a special occasion in the wearer's life and will be passed on to another person later. They are decorated with birds and leaf shapes to suggest the elements of a stylized garden. They are shoes for walking, dancing, or flying. Long pink ties are reminiscent of ballet shoes, the imbricated pattern is European, and the fully beaded soles refer to Plains Indian moccasins.

A.Kimberlin Blackburn

Kapaa, Hawaii

M'Lady Lellium

29 x 19 x 1 in.
glass beads laid into thickened acrylic paint on a hand-carved wooden core

M'Lady Lellium is an angel holding the earth in her care. She cares for the planet and all beings that dwell on her. She spreads her wings for uplifting her planet's inhabitants' spirits.

A. Kimberlin Blackburn

Kapaa, Hawaii

Auntie & Big Boy in the Grove

21 x 21 x 15 in.
glass beads laid into thickened acrylic paint on a hand-carved wooden core

Auntie & Big Boy in the Grove is a piece about reveling in the stream that runs through the grove. Auntie is in her muumuu dancing in the streambed, joyously giving thanks for the water—the elixir of life. Big Boy comes to help Auntie and learn her skill of picking herbs. The Grove is a wondrous place where nature abounds and plants of all kinds nurtured by the water seemingly dance with the water's rhythms.

Beth Blankenship and Mary Whiteley

Anchorage and Kenai, Alaska

Carry On

15 x 18 x 6 in.
bead embroidery on card stock glued to thrift store suitcase; lined with machine-quilted cotton fabric;
blown-glass hearts from Glass Eye Studio in Seattle, Washington

The designs on this suitcase are symbolic portraits of the artists, who are sisters. Beth
Blankenship embroidered seed beads onto paper and adhered the paper to the case, which was
a thrift store find. Mary Whiteley machine quilted the lining of the case with colorful threads
and suspended purchased blown-glass hearts across the opening. This piece was originally created for a collaborative, mixed-media exhibition entitled Inside/Outside, in which one sister produced the exterior of an artwork and the other completed the interior.

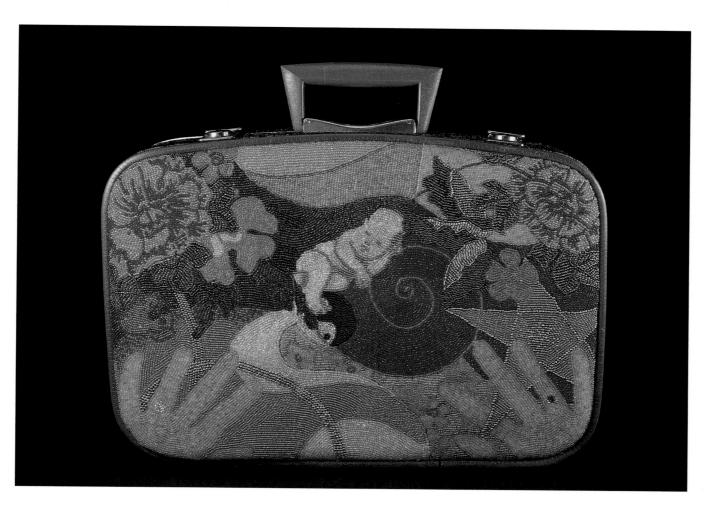

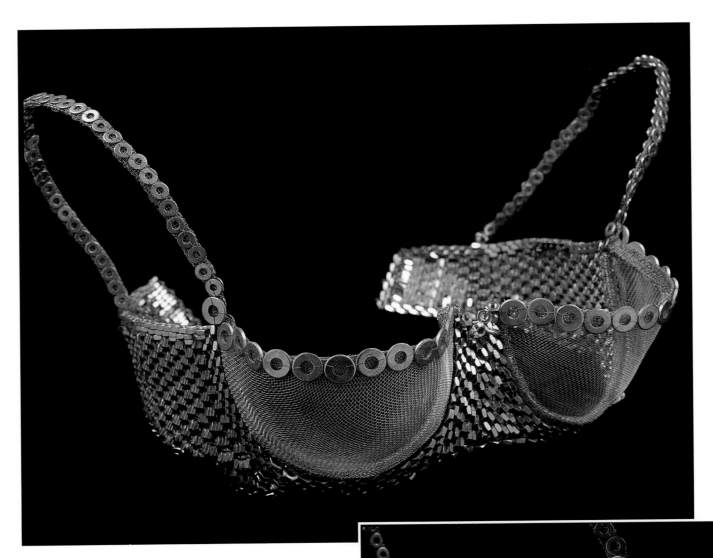

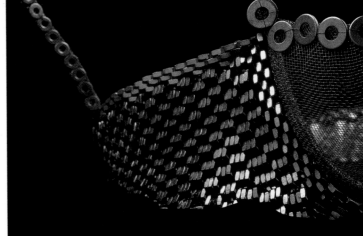

Ingrid Goldbloom Bloch

Needham, Massachusetts

Female Armor

8 x 18 x 12 in.
steel nuts; steel washers; steel screening; fishing line;
steel thread; 1, 2, 3, & 4 drop peyote stitch; embroidery

I love hardware stores. As a little girl, I would accompany my father on his errands and get lost in the aisles imagining all the things I could make from the bits and pieces I came across. Common objects can be very beautiful. By using ordinary items designed for other purposes to create my art, I try to catch the viewers by surprise—bringing a smile to their lips and a question to their minds.

Female Armor is intended to be an ironic, humorous, and beautiful depiction of the "push-up bra."

Photo: Joe Manfredini

Leslie Ciechanowski

Seattle, Washington

Alien Poetry

13 x 16 x 8 in.
right-angle weave; bottle; wire; tubing; copper plate; seed beads

Alien Poetry slowly unfolded over a two-year period. It is playful interplay of color, form, and texture. In an abstract manner, it is the story of an unfolding seed. It's yours to discover.

Photo: Joe Manfredini

Leslie Ciechanowski

Seattle, Washington

Unless

14 x 8 x 8 in.
right-angle weave; fringing; bottle; foam; wire; copper plate; seed beads

Unless was inspired by the Trufula tree in Dr. Seuss's story of the Lorax. It is my tribute to his work, the joyful interplay of his color and shapes, along with a deeper message. Unless . .

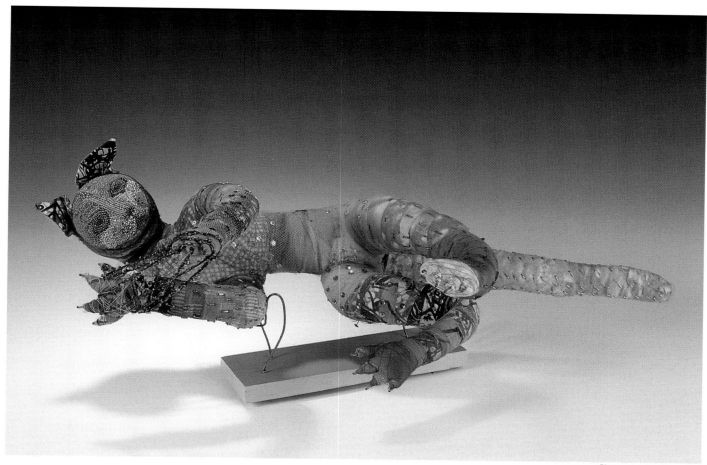

Ann Citron

Alexandria, Virginia

Cat's Cradle

11 x 25 x 18 in.
wrapped wire armature; fiber; beads; wood and wire base

Cats—playful and intelligent creatures that they are—have given us, in *Cat's Cradle*, the feline answer to Chinese Checkers—or maybe even Scrabble.

Photos: provided by artist

Ann Citron

Alexandria, Virginia

Metatron—Soul on Fire

26 x 11 x 18 in.
wrapped wire armature; fiber; beads; enamel on copper, wood base

The angel Metatron is an important figure in the Zohar (a Jewish mystical text from thirteenth-century Spain). According to the Zohar, he is a figure of light and enlightenment in Heaven. In describing his ascent to Heaven, Metatron says, "my flesh was changed into flames ... and the whole of my body into glowing fire," creating a graphic and impressive picture in my imagination.

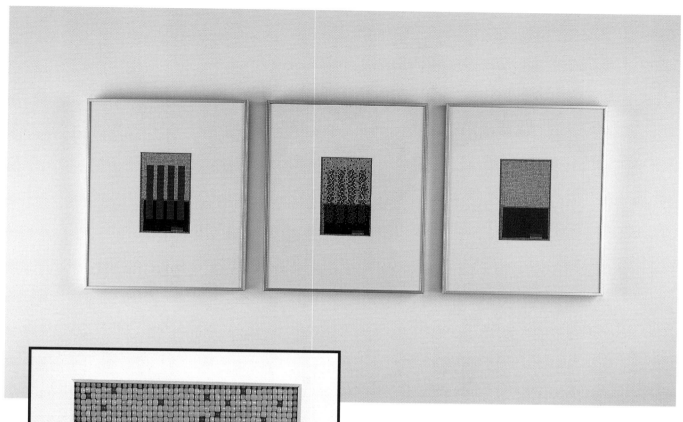

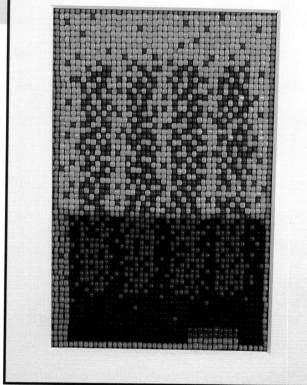

Leland Jay Crow and Barbara L. McGonagle
Oxford, Ohio

Libby Gregory Award for an Ohio Artist

Coming & Going

11 x 32 in.
seed beads; loomwork; Mirrix method

We feel that art in general attempts to capture an image, a thought, a feeling, a moment in time. In this work we attempt to capture the transition of an image, the process of change, the impermanence of objects and ideas.

Marcia Laging Cummings

Lincoln, Nebraska

Jealousy: He said, "That looks just like candy." She said, "Who's Candy?"

14.5 x 10 in.
Japanese and Czech seed beads in various sizes; resin beads; Nymo and Silamide thread; constructed with peyote stitch, square stitch, and right-angle weave

By temperament, I am an improvisational beader. Initial planning consists of broad concepts, frequently as simple as "Guess I'll make a bracelet." One of the drawbacks of not designing a piece prior to beading is that this process makes revision a negative and tiresome experience. To avoid these pitfalls I bead several modular units and later spend "design time" arranging and rearranging the various components. I titled this piece while it was still under construction because "he" actually did come into the room and say, "That looks just like candy." Is it because the large resin bead looks like butterscotch?

Photos: W. Scott Mitchell

Joan Dulla
Chandler, Arizona

Tree of Life

16 x 18 x 18 in.
seed beads; copper wire; self-adhesive bandage; lampworked leaves

We all get our nourishment from the earth. I find that the nourishment of my soul comes from the people I care about. When I isolate myself, part of me dies. By keeping connected with my family and friends, my life flourishes.

Wendy Ellsworth

Quakertown, Pennsylvania

Summer Passion

20 x 3 x 1 in.
fused dichroic glass cabochon; dichroic glass lampworked beads; glass seed beads; dichroic glass button; 24k gold beads; free-form gourd and herringbone stitches

This necklace is an expression of summer. I visualize within it the passion and joy that summer brings, clothed in her glorious riot of exuberant growth and fullness. Each bud, each flower cries out: "Look at me! I am beauty! I am life!" How often do we truly stop to observe and appreciate this sumptuous feast for the senses? And how is it a mirror for the color-full beauty that lies buried like a treasure within us all?

Photos: provided by artist

Jo Ann Feher

Seattle, Washington

Hi Jack

8 x 4 x 1 in.
peyote stitch (hollow three-dimensional); seed beads; strung beads

As a knitter I never hoarded yarn. When I sew, I buy fabric as I
need it. Seed beads are different. I cannot resist a color that is new,
or a finish that is different. To me, seed beads have the appeal of
small jewels or tiny pieces of candy. I take pleasure in having them
near me.

I am amazed at what I can create with a needle, some thread,
and my beads. They talk to me, and things go well when I listen.
My work, light and whimsical in nature, reflects my happiness
while beading.

Photos: provided by artist

Linda Fifield

McKee, Kentucky

Fire on the Mountain

6 x 3.5 in.
*wood vessel turned on a lathe; Czech glass beads; ancient netting stitch
(gourd stitch, diagonal weave); three-dimensional ruffle*

The dark, rich loam of the forest floor, the lush, green leaves of
plants and trees—add to this a forest fire. As a child, watching a
fiery ribbon of flame "snake" up the hills of our Appalachian country home created a lasting impression. I've worked on different
"Earth" design vessels for over twenty years. The three-dimensional
flame-colored bead ribbon transformed this "Earth" vessel into *Fire
on the Mountain.*

Susan Etcoff Fraerman

Highland Park, Illinois

Flight Shoe, Shoe Number Nine

5 x 8 x 2 in.
glass seed beads; feathers; wood; nylon thread; found object; off-loom bead weaving; right-angle weave; applied beads

The creation of *Flight Shoe*, the ninth shoe in a series, took hundreds of hours as individual beads were chosen for color, texture, and reflective quality and woven to the next without a pattern or graph. The wooden vintage last, which served as my armature, felt wonderful to hold and spoke to me of another time and place.

As a teenager, I spent several postoperative months bound in long plaster leg casts. *Flight Shoe* embodies my fantasy of a life of movement without constraint; movement without pain or the pull of gravity. My fascination with shoes and the luminous beauty of beads continues.

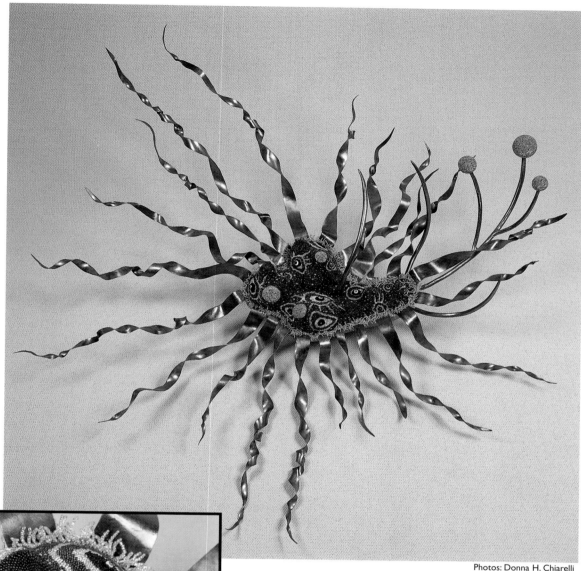

Photos: Donna H. Chiarelli

Kim Z. Franklin

with metalwork by Kim Z. & Michael Franklin
West Chester, Pennsylvania

My Dementia

48 x 54 x 10 in.
*sculptural peyote stitch over hand-molded clay and wood
understructure framed in steel metalwork with peyote-
stitched orb embellishments*

For me, art is a form of supremely delicate awareness, a lifelong process of creativity finding a sense of answer to life's hardest questions. Internal images are my wellspring and unite me to the physical world; therefore I rely strictly on memory images and/or visualization to draw inspiration for my artwork. These images usually manifest themselves in symbolic form and have become mechanisms for understanding the world around me while simultaneously communicating this understanding to others. Inherently they depict myth, legend, dream, and imagination, transcending ordinary thought in a new awareness, with the creative goal to make known the unknown.

Photos: provided by artist

Patty Gallagher
Pittsburgh, Pennsylvania

"Are You Being Served?"

12 x 13 x 12 in.
found objects sewn on vintage bra

Beads are fascinating and compelling. They speak to me about issues like acquisition, wealth, and display. I like to create beads from found objects, not necessarily round or "bead-like," and to stretch the definition of "bead." *"Are You Being Served?"* is about giving again and again without needing to get something back—the Zen of habitual behavior. All these gifts to others blossom like giant flowers. Only on closer inspection can they be seen as hands.

Photo: Melinda Holden

Ana Garcia

Chula Vista, California

Ablaze

18 x 5 in.
seed beads; delica beads; right-angle weave; multiple layers of spiked fringe

This necklace is about warmth, movement, and illumination. It's as though it gently draws warmth from the wearer and moves it through each individual strand, lighting each point.

Photo: Melinda Holden

Ana Garcia

Chula Vista, California

Juror's Award

Self-Portrait: Silence

7 x 7 x 9 in.
seed beads; styrofoam; clay; leather; right-angle weave; brick stitch; fringe

It was important to me to create an accurate representation of myself. To keep the dimensions of the features true, I used a clay impression of my face. Right-angle weave provided a pliable beaded fabric to cover the face. I used brick stitch, a tighter, more rigid weave, to attain the curvature needed for the eyes. Many, many strands of fringe were attached to strips of right-angle weave, which were then stitched together.

Photos: provided by artist

Laura Massie Goldberg

Highland Park, Illinois

End Table Base

22 x 12 x 12 in.
seed beads; embellishment beads; vintage glass buttons; bakelite buttons;
peyote stitch

This table base has been an on-again-off-again two-year labor of
love. I began with the tabletop and worked my way down the sides.
Each part created the next, and, thankfully, came together at the base.

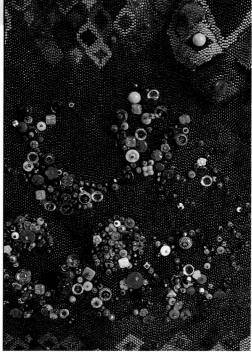

Judi Goolsby

Austin, Texas

La Virgen de las Americas

82 x 48 in.
hand-dyed; discharged; over-dyed; stamped; silk-screened; foiled; machine- and hand-quilted; cut up; stitched back together; hand-stitched shisha mirrors; glass seed beads; antique beads and embellishments; appliqué; 109 beaded quilts

I love color! I love the idea of a piece of white cloth, pristine, open to endless possibilities. My work takes direction from the dye patterns as a springboard and moves to deeper imagery by layering paint, found objects, and especially beads. If in doubt—bead it down! My inspiration comes from deep within, people I've known, places I've traveled, and spiritual imagery mixed with folk art. I hope people who view my work will always have something to think about, something to question, and something to make them smile.

Stephenie Goodwin

Madison, Wisconsin

Jurors' Award

Untitled

3.5 x 9 x 11 in.
glass beads; crochet

My inspiration is drawn from the environment and the fashion industry. My beadwork is created through the manipulation of everyday wearable objects into one-of-a-kind pieces. *Untitled* draws on the Elizabethan period, when men and women wore lavish handmade lace ruffs around their necks. In contrast, women now show off necklaces encrusted with jewels. I decided to create a work embodying both these fashions. I strung beautiful, jewel-toned glass beads and then crocheted them to create a textile similar to that of lace, in an inverted version of the Elizabethan ruff.

Valorie Harlow

Chanhassen, Minnesota

On The Prowl

12 x 18 x 8 in.
seed beads; peyote stitch; right-angle weave

Dogs love adventure. I think that dogs would love to own rocket mobiles. They could zoom around town with their tongues hanging out and their noses in the wind, searching for treats or companions to share the day. I know that Konyak, our Siberian Husky, would have loved it because every chance he got he would be off on a run seeking out new places to explore. This piece is in memory of Konyak and his adventuresome spirit, and his ability to return safely home after an hour or two of private fun.

Valorie Harlow

Chanhassen, Minnesota

On Dragon's Wings

12 x 16 x 6 in.
seed beads; buttons; found teapot; peyote stitch; right-angle weave; fringe technique

I would like to have a pet dragon to take me on whatever adventure my heart desires. Perhaps the dragon represents the imagination and the unlimited possibilities we all have within us.

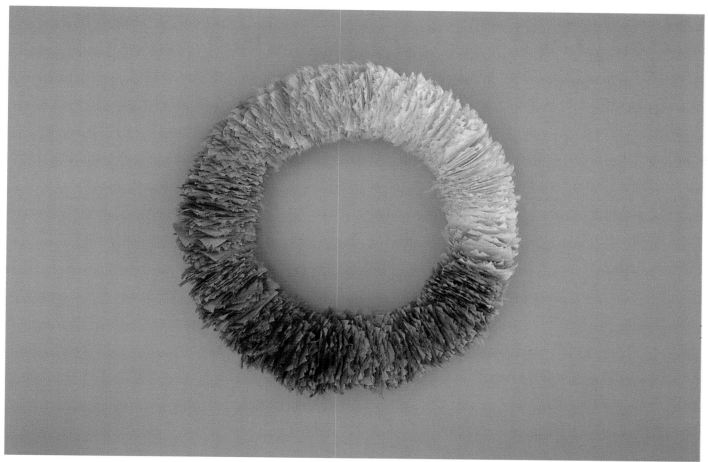

Photos: provided by artist

Ursula Hofmann
Nuremburg, Germany

Necklace

15 x 7 in.
hand-dyed silk, torn, cut, and frayed; 2,400 silk squares
on elastic band

I am exploring the special qualities of a certain
nonprecious material not normally used for jewelry.
I try to lend it a different kind of preciosity by the
way I exploit its qualities and by the use of color.

Nancy Terry Hooten

Savannah, Georgia

Juror's Award

I'm All Right

14 x 22 in.
seed beads embroidered on canvas; couching; netting; peyote stitch

This subject came from a vivid dream occurring a year following my mother's death. It represents my mother's life, death, and her existence in an afterlife. When she appeared in my dream, so young and healthy, I was surprised and expressed delight in seeing her. I told her how worried I had been during her last illness, to which she replied, "I know you were, that's why I wanted you to know that I'm all right."

Photos: Jim Holmes

Nancy Terry Hooten

Savannah, Georgia

A Present for Hester

6 x 8 x 3 in.
bead weaving on loom; embroidered seed beads on
canvas; mounted on foam core in wooden box

A Present for Hester is a celebration for an underap-
preciated woman in literature. Many women
throughout history have received similar presents
from a man, resulting in pain, joy, wonder, and
amazement. But in all instances, receiving this gift is
a life-altering experience.

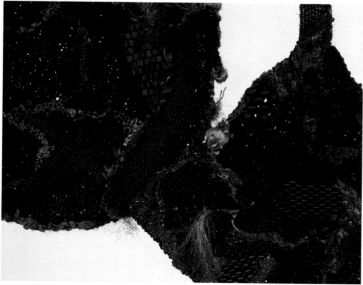

Karen Hoyt
Portland, Oregon

Journey

20 x 20 x 3 in.
seed beads of various sizes; fiber; peyote, brick, and ndebele stitch

Beadwork is a game with no particular rules—a puzzle that must be solved. I have an obsession with solving puzzles: the pieces of the beadwork puzzle need to fit together to form a solution that is visually pleasing. The beginning seems to be a vague idea. The work spontaneously changes along the way, as the beads have a mind of their own, forcing me to be the catalyst.

Journey is a portrayal of the path so many people close to me have taken in an attempt to find a way out of the darkness of serious illness.

David L. Johnson

Chicago, Illinois

Persona

7 x 15 in.
computer image transfer (original drawing and photography); beads; waxed linen; painted felt carpet pad; 1/2-inch screen

Folk/outsider and ethnographic art inspire my mixed-media work. The work deals essentially with transformation: the alchemy of making thoughts, feelings, and subconscious images into things, and of using base materials—plant and animal fibers, wood, metal, glass, stone, and paper—to reference the calmer and more enchanted world that lies parallel to our often hurried reality. Most of my work includes photography and computer design using images from the urban environment. The photography celebrates what Thomas Moore calls "the re-enchantment of everyday life" by looking for beauty in unlikely and frequently overlooked spaces.

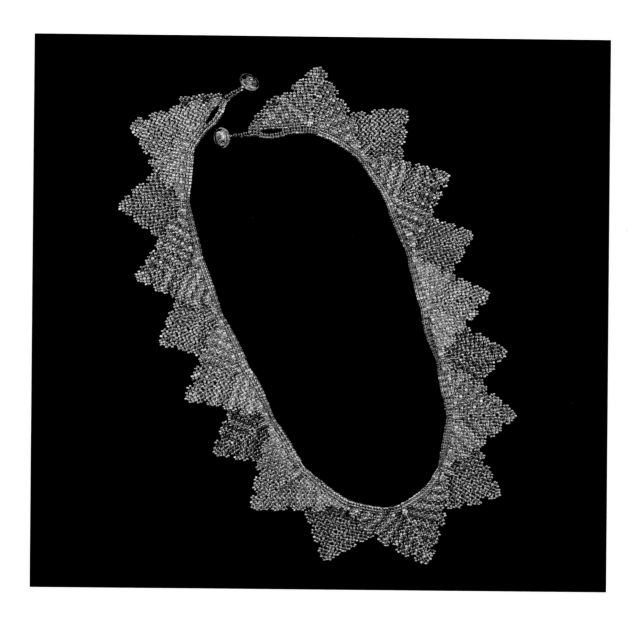

Jacqueline Johnson

Yonkers, New York

Eyelet Necklace

21 x 1 in.
delicas; gold electroplated charlottes; nymo thread; dichroic beads by Paula Radke; right-angle weave

From childhood sewing and knitting to a profession of creating woven design for interiors, my creative pursuits have revolved around making, decorating, and using cloth. Now I am exploring the "textile" quality of beads: the drape of a design, the texture of the surface, the stretch of different stitches, and the durability of a construction. Currently my focus is on pattern and bias in ribbon constructions. With the glorious array of colors and transparency, the ease of set-up, and the personal choice and control from beginning to end, spending time with beads is sheer pleasure.

Jacqueline Johnson
Yonkers, New York

Curves Necklace

20 x 1 in.
delicas; nymo thread; antique glass button; right-angle weave

Ella Johnson-Bentley

Juneau, Alaska

Not So Straight Laced

1.5 x 2 x 4 in.
single-needle right-angle weave; peyote stitch; seed beads; ultrasuede; dyed cotton for stuffing

There is no hidden meaning or message involved in my beadwork. I find great fulfillment when I can interpret an idea, a line drawing, or a flat picture as a three-dimensional object. I am particularly interested in men's used shoes, as they have such great character, and I love to recreate them with beads. I scale them to not more than four inches in any direction. If my little shoes make you smile, then I have achieved my goal.

Ella Johnson-Bentley

Juneau, Alaska

Easy Strider

4 x 2 x 4 in.
single-needle right-angle weave; peyote stitch; straight
stitch; seed beads; small key rings; antique nailhead
beads; ultrasuede; cotton stuffing

Bette Kelley

Yellow Springs, Ohio

The Secret Life of Oaks

15 x 5 in.
broad collar techniques: ladders; horizontal netting; fringe; overlays; backbars; braiding

About four years ago I was taking the dogs for their usual walk in the Glen. It was fall and I was looking at leaves on the ground as we went along our normal path. Suddenly I found a leaf of the most beautiful rose color with small patches of tangerine and some brown spots. I realized it was an oak leaf, but the big surprise was when I turned it over. The "right" side was yellow, with some brown and green—totally unremarkable. The beauty lay in the secret side. I began the necklace and finished the top, then put it aside to "age" as I figured out what to do next. In the recent past I have become obsessed with trees and leaves. It took four tries, but I finally achieved an oak leaf and a fringe that celebrates "the secret life of oaks."

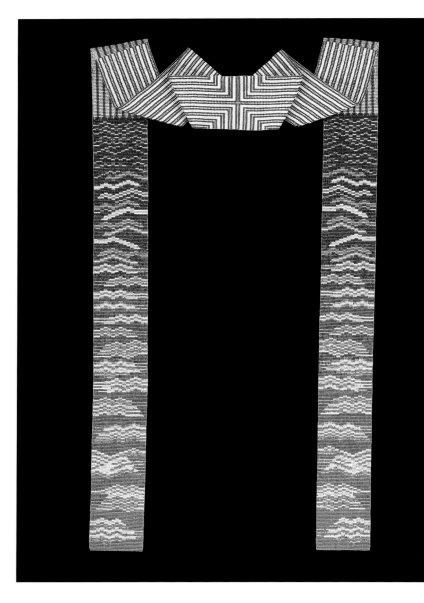
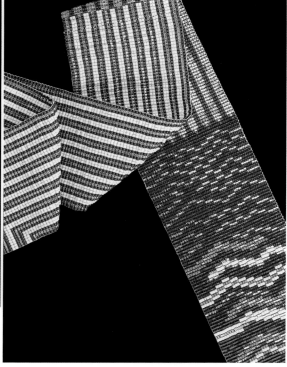

Katherine Korff

Fort Gratiot, Michigan

Waters of Baptism—In Memoriam—Liturgical Stole

72 x 2 in.
loom-woven glass seed beads

Water is elemental to life. A tiny glass bead reflects light in much the same manner as a drop of water. As light plays on water, the central image of the cross moves around the stole, flowing into the quiet, distant water which swells on the tide of faith.

In the year 2000, I lost my best friend. Judith Morgan brought humor, balance, and perception to her friends and to the hundreds of art students at Athens High School whom she exposed to the possibilities of the world. She was a deliciously irritating thorn in the side of those friends and students, and her laughter was a balm that soothed and renewed their spirits.

With much gratitude for the love of art and life that we shared, I dedicate this work.

Photos: provided by artist

Connie Lehman

Elizabeth, Colorado

leaf-love, luna

5 x 5 in.
bead embroidery and needle punch on silk noil; sequins; steel cut and glass seed beads; cotton; silk and metallic thread

I love the decorated surface. I love the fact that artists have always been unable not to decorate. I think the whole process is absolute alchemy, mystery, history—the feeling that this comes right out of your bones and your blood and your ancient brain and blasts through your eyes and hands, and nobody can ever mess with it. It's yours. That's why I do art.

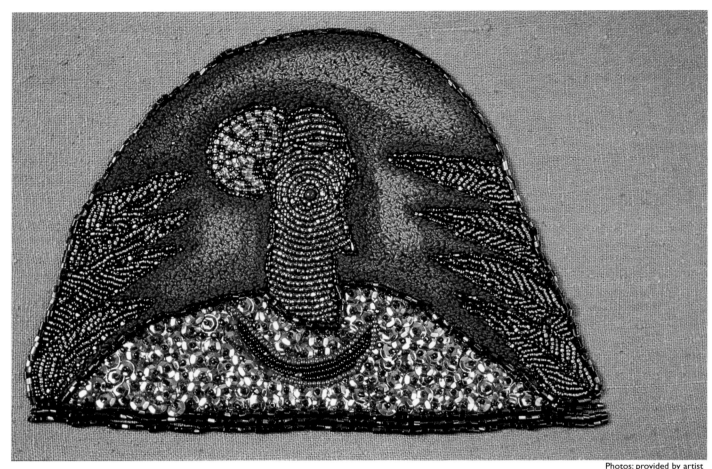

Photos: provided by artist

Connie Lehman

Elizabeth, Colorado

leaf-love, lilly

4 x 6 in.
bead embroidery and needle punch on silk noil;
sequins; steel cut and glass seed beads; lapis; cotton
and metallic thread

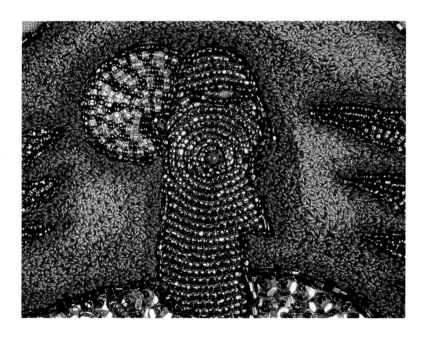

Photos: provided by artist

Connie Lehman
Elizabeth, Colorado

leaf-love, lila

5 x 6 in.
bead embroidery and needle punch on silk noil;
sequins; glass seed beads; jet beads; turquoise; cotton
and metallic thread

Laura Leonard

Minneapolis, Minnesota

Summer in Fargo

5 x 6 x 6 in.
fabric-wrapped wire armature; peyote stitch; "snow" is glued beads on styrofoam

My work celebrates everyday moments of life in a whimsical way. Fargo is one place that has worse weather than we do in Minneapolis. This information helps me through our winters. I wanted to show how easy it can be to enjoy winter by ignoring it. My main goal is to delight the viewer, to bring a smile. The next goal, a very close second, is to buy groceries.

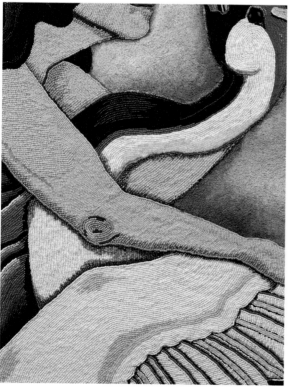

Lisa Lew

Silt, Colorado

The Manchurian

37 x 29 in.
seed and bugle beads embroidered on ultrasuede; oil paint and oil pastels mixed with sand

Although I have been working with beads for over twenty-five years, only the last ten have been devoted to exploring the creation of painterly images with beads—either through embroidery, or through work on a loom. The spark and texture of beads adds more to a piece than I can achieve with just paint.

Barbara Lewis

Evanston, Illinois

Rainbow Fish Amulet Bag Neckpiece

fish: 5 x 3.5 x 1 in.; back: 4 x 7 in.
delica beads; electrostatically plated small metal fish and lead
fishing sinkers; fishing lure; peyote stitch; netting

I learned to bead using 11° delica beads. The liquid feel and
look of those small, shiny beads seemed the perfect medium
for a fish. Researching fish, I found that rainbow fish have
subtle colors that please me. With a shortened tail, the proportions work well aesthetically. I deliberately sought a realistic look recognizable to people who fish.

A neckpiece should be interesting front and back, so lead sinkers add weight and texture to the back netting with the caught fish. The fishing lure and (unseen) small fish
being swallowed by the large one remind me of life and amuse me.

62

Haley Licata

Highland Park, Illinois

Great Chain of Being

6 x 6 in.
seed beads; tubular and flat peyote stitch; embellished with caddis weave stitch

Each bead and link in my *Great Chain of Being* necklace expresses a visual dialogue of relationships, unity, and interdependency. What is whole on one level—the bead—is merely reduced to part of a larger whole at the next level—the link—representing the beads' individual, yet communal, identities and the hierarchy of all forms of life and matter.

Donna L. Lish

Clinton, New Jersey

Demon Seeds

10 x 3 x 3 in.
glass; metal; plastic; machine-knitted; crocheted

Sparked by a memory of a 1977 sci-fi movie,
Demon Seeds embodies a sinister impression of
nature gone awry—mutation and chaos. This was
my first influence, as I often commence a work
with deep contemplation, honed by inescapable
realism. Yet, this sculpture may also tickle the out-
landish whimsical notion that such seeds, with fins,
nodules, and prickly bracts, could ever spawn any
sort of life. More often than not, my work results
in a lighthearted perception—not as the naughty
prank I initially envision. Onward optimism!

Eleanor Lux
Eureka Springs, Arkansas

Fading Night

5 x 25 x 11 in.
seed beads; bugle beads; rock crystals

After a month of camping last year, this piece evolved. I found I frequently woke too early and had to wait patiently for the first rays of sun, so I could see to work again.

Expressing my thoughts and feelings in a visual way has always been the most relaxing and/or exciting way for me to belong in this world.

I've worked in many mediums, but textiles have kept my heart warm and glass has kept my eyes alive. I did spend many years working by day in stained glass and by night as a weaver. When I began to blend the two together in beading, I finally felt comfortable and wanted to stay there forever. Bringing light and reflection to softness and movement made it possible for me to say everything.

Jennifer Maestre

Concord, Massachusetts

Most Innovative Use of the Medium

3 to 1 Twist

17 x 10 x 10 in.
pencils stubs, all sharpened by hand; peyote stitch

I consider myself a sculptor first, a beader second. Beading is my diversion; however, the beading techniques I have learned have enabled me to expand the formal and structural vocabulary of my sculptural work. I use industrially produced materials (nails and pencils) to create forms reminiscent of the organic shapes of animals and nature. This piece is part of a series originally based on the form and function of the sea urchin.

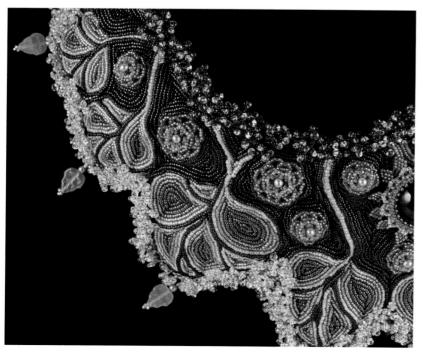

Laura Jean McCabe
Noank, Connecticut

Sunflower

15 x 12 in.
glass seed beads; star quartz cabochon;
Czech glass; freshwater pearls; ultrasuede;
embroidery; peyote stitch; lacy stitch;
embellishment

This beaded collar is constructed of glass seed beads and a stone cabochon stitched onto ultrasuede using various beadweaving techniques. My design inspiration was drawn from the Karlsplatz station in Vienna designed by Otto Wagner in 1894–99, which features elegant Art Nouveau renderings of sunflowers and leaves. Art Nouveau design, with its endless fluidity and elegance, lends itself well to beadwork.

Particular attention was given in this piece to the closure mechanism at center back, which is composed of two beaded vines of berries (freshwater pearls) that tie over the hidden silver clasp.

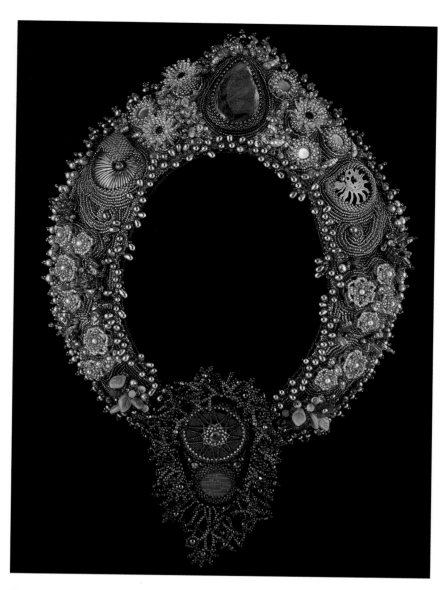

Laura Jean McCabe

Noank, Connecticut

Conflict of Interest

10 x 14 x 2 in.
glass seed beads; freshwater pearls; Czech glass; labradorite; pyratized ammonites; mother of pearl; rainbow obsidian; cat's eye (shell); computer circuitry board; leather; Bali silver clasps; embroidery; peyote stitch; lacy stitch; branch fringe; embellishment

This beaded collar is constructed of glass beads, pearls, and stones stitched onto leather using various beadweaving techniques. The main portion of the collar represents the natural world in all its vibrancy. Sea anemones, shells, and brilliant blue labradorite represent the oceans. Flowers and berries represent the land. The removable centerpiece contains a section of computer circuitry board, representing technology. Dead flowers surrounding the computer chip suggest the negative impact of rapid technological advancement on the natural world. The wearer of this collar, representing mankind, stands at the center of this struggle between technology and nature.

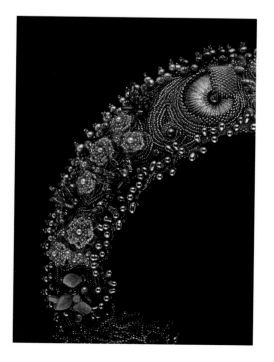

Ann Tevepaugh Mitchell

Wayland, Massachusetts

The Birdwatcher

15 x 8 x 6
glass beads; silamide thread; two rocks

As a classically trained artist, I use glass beads to create visual brilliance and emotional intensity. The light, energy, surprise, and humor of beads contribute to the expression of my figures. I use no armatures or patterns; the thread tension locks the beads together. I search for something in nature (a found object, an antique) that can be transformed by integrating it into the beadwork. My figures grow equally from realistic observation and from personal observation. As I work, my concentration is engaged, my skills are challenged, and my life is enriched.

Photos: provided by artist

Ann Tevepaugh Mitchell

Wayland, Massachusetts

Bees of Paradise

6 x 11 x 11
glass beads; antique beads; metal beads; plexiglass
posts; silamide thread

Jennifer Mokren

Green Bay, Wisconsin

Anemone Object

9 x 6 x 6 in.
delica beads; copper; enamel; peyote stitch; electroformed and enameled copper interior

I am interested in the vessel as a container and in what is contained that cannot be seen: more specifically, in the oppositional nature of interior versus exterior. What is seen on the outside of objects often gives no indication of what lies within. My work is a peeling back of materials to reveal the core, a cross-section, or a view through a microscope. Plant biology and found organic objects are a major influence in my work; they motivate my handling of surface, color, and form.

Jennifer Mokren

Green Bay, Wisconsin

Berry Objects

3 x 7 x 4 in.
delica beads, copper; enamel; peyote stitch; electroplated and enameled copper interiors

Photo: provided by artist

Nicole Nagel-Gogolak

Fairfax, California

Little Black Dress

14 x 6 x 4 in.
cocktail straws; floss; commanche weave

I am inspired by the disposable items cast off by our culture. The odd, less-significant bits around us make for very unconventional beads. When the detritus of life is assembled into a larger whole it is transformed. For a dress of quartered cocktail straws or a satchel of diced sponges, the goal is the same: to create something that challenges the boundaries of traditional beadwork, something that tickles your imagination and ultimately causes you to wonder, as you look around, "Is that a bead?"

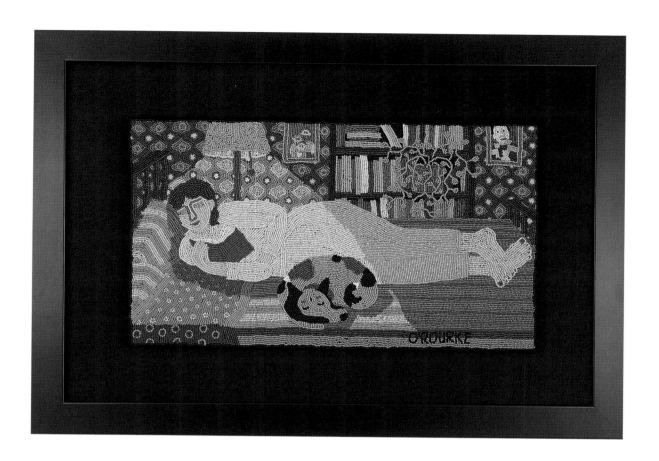

Colleen O'Rourke

Antioch, California

Bedtime Stories

11 x 19 in.
seed beads; embroidery

The day before transferring from Chicago to California I discovered I was pregnant. Once in California I decided not to pursue a job, and imagined this is what people thought was my lifestyle. My reality was quite the opposite. I was constantly ill and miserable. I missed my network of friends and family. This image of relaxing with my dog was my dream. The process of creating this piece did help me relax and discover some humor in my situation. It also inspired me to start my next series of mother-and-child-related images.

Colleen O'Rourke

Antioch, California

Pool

9.5 x 5 x 5 in.
off-loom weaving

My beadwork is about self-examination and expression, but also about seeing humor in myself while taking delight in the action of others. My inspiration is drawn from feelings, dreams, conflicts, politics, and attitudes, which I translate into characters in a particular setting. The beads become a narration that allows the viewer to take in each element and decide what the story is about so it can be related to her/his own experience. *Pool* was inspired by a simple thought that developed into this image. The diversity of beads allows me to present art that is mysterious, serious, sarcastic, or humorous.

Betty Pan

New Rochelle, New York

Robe of Longevity

14 x 14 in.
delica beads; square stitch

I am interested in costumes of different cultures. Since I started beading, I have made a series of Chinese, Japanese, and Native American miniature costumes. The woven beads resemble Chinese and Japanese brocade. I especially like to use Native American and Chinese symbols for the design of beadwork. The motif for this piece is the Chinese symbol for longevity, which is of utmost importance to the Chinese.

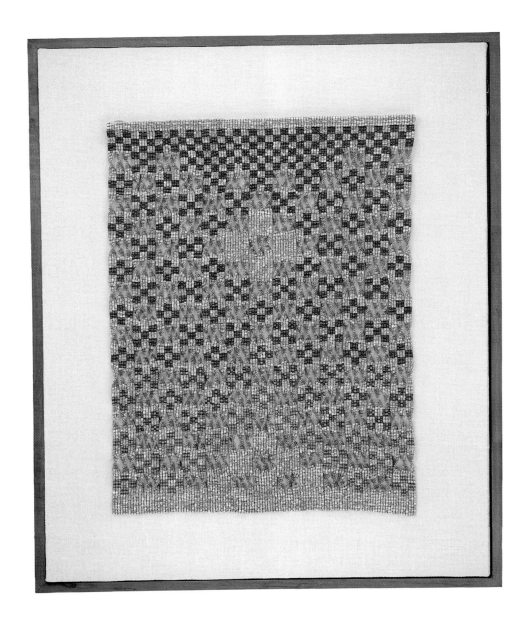

Betty Pan

New Rochelle, New York

Hopscotch with a Twist

20 x 16 in.
triangle beads; square stitch

Since I started working with Toho triangle beads, I
have been able to give dimension to my beadwork. I
like the texture of the beads when woven. I am
excited that the triangle beads are bigger, which
enables me to create bigger work.

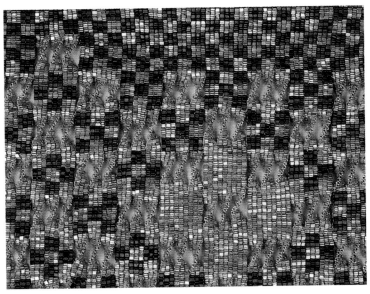

Photo: provided by artist

Karen Paust

York, Pennsylvania

Jack in the Pulpit

6 x 5 x 2 in.
glass seed beads; thread; wire; sterling silver pin; variations on peyote stitch

For the past eleven years, I have been creating nontraditional beaded art inspired by my experiences, dreams, nature, and everyday life. I chose this medium because beadwork mirrors the cell-like quality of life and how everything in the universe is physically and symbolically connected. My work has evolved into increasingly complex and intricate beaded interpretations of botanical and zoological forms and is mostly three dimensional, ranging from wearable art to large sculptural pieces.

My goal as an artist is to explore and to expand the possibilities of beadwork. The positive response to my work is a sign of growing acceptance of beadwork as fine art. Through my work, I intend to inspire people to observe nature, to spark them into thinking about their own connection to their environment, and to introduce them to the beauty and cell-like qualities of beads.

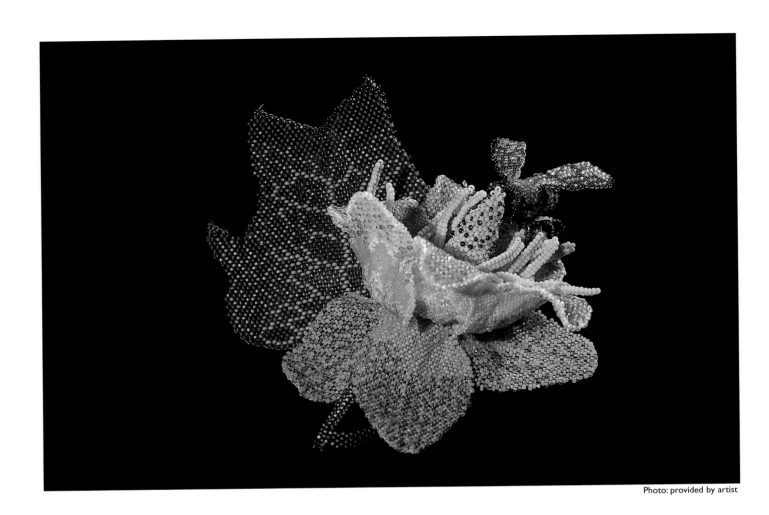

Photo: provided by artist

Karen Paust

York, Pennsylvania

Tulip Tree and Honey Bee

4 x 4 x 3 in.
glass seed beads; thread; wire; wood; sterling silver pin; variations on peyote stitch

Christy Puetz
Cave Creek, Arizona

Self-Awareness Quilt

33 x 23 in.
seed beads sewn onto Aida cloth; laminated pictures; fabric people

I cover surfaces with color, texture, and honesty. It is my hope to make compelling personal images. I am describing powerful thoughts in a beautiful and mysterious manner. My art is in the world to charm and seduce as well as to challenge and offend. Reactions and conversation are important benefits I receive in return as a bonus.

Photos: provided by artist

Lorraine Randecker

Falls Church, Virginia

Ode to Wassily

16 in.
polymer clay, millefiore technique

In the small community where I grew up, art was considered extravagant, exotic. Personal adornment was spare, functional. But that didn't stop me. Later, college brought exposure to large-city galleries and museums. My major was in science, my minor was in art, especially as jewelry. I progressed from seeds and feathers to necklaces of bookmarks, tea infusers, and my mother's curlers. I've worked over forty years as a scientist, with scant formal art training. But always my first love is art and its expression in personal adornment.

Helen Banes introduced me to polymer clay at the Torpedo Factory in Alexandria, Virginia, and I became addicted. No longer limited by "found" objects, I could fashion my own beads from a facile medium. I love making large pieces, and my inspiration comes from Pier Voulkos, Tony Duquette, and Wassily Kandinski. I try to incorporate a bit of color, a little caprice, and a lot of flourish. You put my necklace on and say: "Look at me—I'm having fun."

Photos: provided by artist

Linda J. Somlai

Racine, Wisconsin

Tidal Pool II

57 x 41 in.
glass seed and bugle beads; semiprecious beads and stones; antique metal fringes and trims; copper and brass knitted wire stitched to painted and foiled canvas

This piece is for anyone open to experiencing what is in front of them. Seed beads are my primary medium, providing many opportunities for gradual color change. The various beads and materials, such as antique metallic trim, change the interplay between light and texture. Glass provides a reflective surface that shifts dimensions of color and depth as light bounces off the piece.

The idea for the piece came from a reflective moment along Charleston Beachway in Rhode Island. Walking with my husband one summer morning along Block Island Sound, I strolled the cliffs beside tidal pools, mini waterways left behind by the tide. Each pool was a gift of light glistening across the sand. I started working on this surface with a pencil sketch, then solid flat beaded areas, and finished with dimensional areas of woven wire. That day, the tidal pool captured me and I wanted to share it with others.

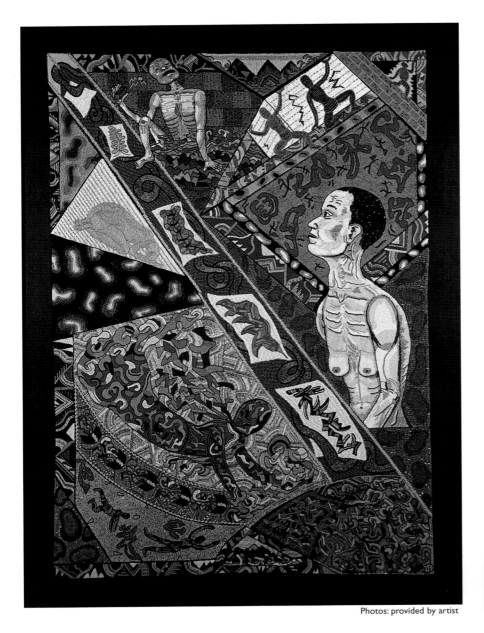

Photos: provided by artist

The Best in Contemporary Beadwork 2002

Linda J. Somlai

Racine, Wisconsin

Juror's Award

360 Degrees Unknown

65 x 49 in.
glass seed and bugle beads stitched to muslin; mounted to gessoed canvas

This piece is meant to connect as a circular, rather than linear, story. Seed and bugle beads offer vast color possibilities. I began the piece where the figure stands, as a reflection of internal noise and confusion. This narrative reads counterclockwise, as imprisoned thoughts are released in stillness and ultimate freedom. What happens when we step outside and connect with the richness of this stream of life? This piece is a personal symbology. Each bead is strung in one-to-two-inch segments, stitched to muslin, and then worked in two-by-two-foot sections, reconnected and mounted to canvas.

This piece comes from a deep place of unknowing that compels me to do something. The action of picking up beads is what I do.

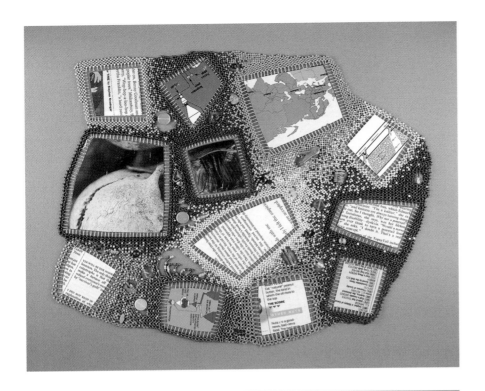

Teresa Sullivan

Portland, Oregon

Particle Flow

13 x 11 in.
seed beads; glass beads; buttons; laminated magazine cutouts; freeform right-angle weave

Particle Flow began spontaneously. The magazine slices had been used as packing material in a large shipment of boxes, and I took sections from them that fit in with the theme I'd been using in other beadwork projects. This theme involves unseen connections such as radio waves, solar winds, and our "collective unconscious." Particle Flow offers both prosaic and mysterious examples of these themes: industrial conveyors, world travelers, TV listings, silent weaponry, Muzak, peanut butter. Each magazine slice is surrounded by a single color of beads that merges into the colors of its neighbors.

Photos: Azadian

James Edward Talbot

Austin, Texas

Anger and Grief

35 x 18 x 7 in.
*seed bead fringe; stone; wood; fluorescent
light; plexiglass mirror*

In the last thirty years I've incorporated millions of beads into my art. When I see the effect that the accumulation of thousands of richly colored, sparkling pieces of glass has on people, I realize that I'm deep in the middle of an ancient spiritual tradition. Apart from their religious, monetary, and decorative uses throughout the ages, beads, I have come to see, are above all magical. People have always sensed that.

Photo: provided by artist

Laura Willits

Seattle, Washington

Seattle, Washington

Best of Show

City North of Home

16 x 18 in.
loom-woven glass seed beads

I like water towers and I like things lit from below, so I made this piece.
The water tower is based on one in a town north of my parents'
house, hence the name.

Photo: provided by artist

Laura Willits

Seattle, Washington

Family Portrait

13 x 16 in.
loom-woven glass seed beads

This piece is called "Family Portrait" because the positions and illuminations of the buildings in it mirror the situation among three members of one of my families at the time I did the drawing.

Photo: provided by artist

Laura Willits

Seattle, Washington

Greetings from Sleepy Eye

13 x 10 in.
loom-woven seed beads

I glimpsed a contractor's trailer on a job site one night. When I
woke up the next day, it looked like this when I drew it.

Cindy Wrobel

St. Louis, Missouri

Grecian Urn with Attitude

13 x 11 x 6.5 in.
wire; beads; rock

My beaded wire sculptural objects reflect an interest in world cultures, art history, nature, and symbols. Each piece finds a balance between tradition and my imagination. They are a creative journey from beginning to finish, and offer me an opportunity to experiment and to be surprised. My art is a celebration of life.

Grecian Urn with Attitude began with my appreciation of the varied and elegant urn forms made throughout Europe. I allowed those classic proportions to break loose, creating new energy and character. *Grecian Urn with Attitude* is coated in a beaded treasure of texture, pattern, color, and fun.

Betsy Youngquist

Rockford, Illinois

Dream Cow

8 x 12 in.
acrylic ink painting on watercolor board; glued glass beads; found objects; finished with a coat of acrylic glass medium

My work consists of intimate representational paintings embellished with beads and found objects. The themes of my paintings are transformations of personal experiences. Cultural mythology and iconography help to support the narrative within each piece. I work with figures of people, animals, and mythological creatures in a setting full of color and fantasy. A symbolic narrative is created as people are metaphorically transformed and animals are given human attributes. This work reflects my interest in the intersection of humans, animals, and mythology, as well as my belief that wisdom can be found through attending to the living world around us.

Betsy Youngquist
Rockford, Illinois

High Horse on Bear Mountain

19 x 15 in.
acrylic ink painting on watercolor board; glued glass
beads; found objects; finished with a coat of acrylic glass
medium

Sage Zering
Richmond, California

Conch Shell

5 x 12 x 7 in.
glass seed beads; peyote stitch; styrofoam internal base

In this piece my intention is to bring together the complex shape of the conch shell with the transparency and graceful curves of the seed bead fabric. The grand size of the shell allows you to concentrate more on the patterns and colors of the shell and not the beads themselves. I have always been attracted to the transparency and stained glass qualities beads have. The mix of colors reflect my visions of summertime sun-washed sandy beaches and golden hillsides. The flowing pattern gradually getting darker and brighter towards the inside of the shell creates movement and accentuates every curve. The shell has a very fluid colorful pattern that resembles the turbulent flow of water.

Working on this piece was challenging and followed a natural progression in my work. The structure, design, and color always seem to evolve into something greater each time. Beads are without a doubt my favorite medium to work with.

"...style. is fashion, home, beauty... it's all there. it's fantastic."

Helen Ziga
St. Davids, Pennsylvania

Smarten Suit

12 x 10 in.
beads; paint; magazine on paper

In the pieces *Smarten Suit* and *Passage* the materials I chose were women's fashion magazines, beads, and paint. These pieces attempt to draw parallels between two centuries that are often perceived as being moral and social opponents.

In nineteenth-century America and western Europe, it was common for wealthy women to spend a good deal of time consulting fashion plates and using those images in crafts. This concept of leisure inspired my method of painting used in these two works. I chose traditional materials that have been very popular in craft today and before the turn of the twentieth century. Beads are substituted for print to provide a colorful rendition of the attire of the portrait on that magazine page.

The resultant flatness of the painted clothing on the model is relief-like, in much the same style the Neoclassical painters adopted in the early and mid-nineteenth century. The visual similarities between contemporary fashion photography of women and the painted portrait by such artists as Rossetti are distinctive and speak about the status of women still today as objects to be viewed and consumed.

Helen Ziga
St. Davids, Pennsylvania

Passage

12 x 10 in.
beads; paint; magazine on paper

Index of Artists

Bead International 2002

Bold indicates award winner

Index of Artwork

Bead International 2002

Index of Sponsors

Bead International 2002

Exhibition Support Provided By:

Byzantium
1088 North High St
Columbus OH 43201
614-291-3130
www.bigbead.com
Sponsor of the Libby Gregory Award for an Ohio Artist

Miyuki Shoji Co., Ltd.
Manufacturers and Suppliers of Glass Beads, Beads & Crafts
www.miyuki-beads.co.jp
Japan

Shipwreck Beads
2500 Mottman Rd, SW
Olympia WA 98512
360-754-2323

The City of Athens
http://ci.athens.oh.us

The Ohio Arts Council
http://www.oac.state.oh.us

Catalog Support Provided By:

Bead and Things
8 North Shafer
Athens OH 45701
BEADS@frognet.net
740-592-6453

The Bead Society of Greater Chicago
PO Box 8103
Wilmette IL 60091-8103
312-458-0519
www.BSGC.org

Great Lakes Beadworkers Guild
PO Box 1639
Royal Oak MI 48068
248-626-6725
www.glbg.org